JERRY LEE LEWIS

A Life from Beginning to End

D1398951

Table of Contents

Introduction

Jerry Lee Lewis was born on September 29, 1935, in the backcountry bayous of Ferriday, Louisiana. His father Elmo was a jack of all trades who did carpentry work as well as small-scale farming on the side, while his mother Mamie mainly took care of the household and the children.

As far back as Jerry could remember, his father was either in jail or actively roving about from one job to another, moving the family from one rundown shanty house to the next. Along with all this hard, manual labor, Elmo apparently also produced alcohol with his brother, which they then turned around and marketed to the locals. No matter what they did, though, the family seemed to always remain dirt poor—a fact that Jerry Lee Lewis realized fairly early in life. He learned as a small child that life was a sink-or-swim existence—sometimes literally so.

When Jerry Lee Lewis was three years old, his father Elmo thought it prudent to teach the boy how to swim. They were cruising through the bayou in a ramshackle boat when Elmo suddenly shoved his boy overboard and began shouting at him to swim. Biographer Rick Bragg played around with the beat-up piano at church, but he never dreamed that he would ever actually have one of his own. His father only had one instruction for his son—now that the family had a piano, he ordered him to "play it." Once they lugged that piano off the truck and into the house, Jerry Lee Lewis didn't hesitate to do just that.

Lewis, along with his cousin of future televangelist fame Jimmy Swaggart, would spend hours at a time pounding those keys. Both of them became quite good, but it was Jerry Lee Lewis who would demonstrate a very unique talent early on. From the get-go, he was able to play entirely by ear, and soon he could play just about anything after hearing it once. Although he was not classically trained, he seemed to automatically know how things should sound. It was this great ear and intuitive sense of musical instinct, coupled with relentless long hours at the keys playing, that would forge his formidable talent.

Although Lewis was for the most part self-taught, he would later admit that he did take one brief piano lesson when he was 12 years old. However, after the piano teacher pulled out a music book and tried to get him to play what he considered "stuff for kids," Lewis made sure that boogie-woogie version of the gospel standard "My God is Real" at an event hosted by the Bible Institute. While the audience absolutely loved his version—as was demonstrated by his peers jumping up and dancing in front of their seats—school administrators were none too pleased. Shortly thereafter, he was kicked out of the school simply for playing a tune that sounded too secular for the tastes of school officials.

The expulsion had the result of sending Jerry Lee Lewis even harder on the track of rock and roll, and after leaving Bible school, he headed back home and hit the club scene harder than ever. Along with all of this clubbing, he also had to make money, and since he wasn't yet being paid enough for his music to make it a full-time profession, that meant he had to take part in a veritable string of odd jobs and manual labor enterprises. He dug ditches, worked in factories, and at one point even tried his luck as a door-to-door salesman, hawking sewing machine equipment.

Desperate to make sales, Lewis was not entirely honest with his customers. He would tell them that they would need to put down little to no money to get the sewing machine but would neglect to mention that they would be stuck with hefty payments in the months to come. It would that Lewis had left Jane in. This resulted in a quite accurately described shotgun wedding, in which Lewis married the girl even though he was technically still married to Dorothy. He then divorced his first wife a couple of weeks later.

Much like his first, Lewis' second marriage was far from ideal. Even after their first child—Jerry Lee Lewis Jr.—was born in November of 1953, the couple would continually argue and bicker. According to Lewis, it was so bad that many of the altercations became violent. He never shied away from these chilling details and would later recall that his wife Jane "hit like a man." According to Lewis, she even threw him down a flight of stairs one time. The couple had moved into an apartment, and the neighbors that lived around them could attest to the arguments as well as the never-ending stream of arbitrary objects that were hurled across the room and even out into the parking lot.

Jerry Lee Lewis, in the meantime, was still looking for his next big break in the music industry and made an effort to audition for the famed Louisiana Hayride, which had served as a mainstay for country music artists. They couldn't quite handle his jumping and jiving piano, however, and declined to invite him on the show. It was after this rejection that Lewis began to look outside of Louisiana. For a time, he headed off to Nashville and tried to get on the Grand Ole Opry, but even here, he was running into more or less the same problems. His piano style often wasn't appreciated or even fully understood in the country music mecca. To his great disgust, Jerry Lee Lewis was, in fact, repeatedly told to put down the piano and pick up a guitar.

As disheartening as this might have been for Lewis, it's easy to understand why the folks down in Nashville might have taken this stance. All one has to do is consider just how ubiquitous guitar strumming was in Nashville then—and in many ways still is now—and it's understandable why they might have preferred a guitar player. At any rate, the end result was the same, leaving a very frustrated and disillusioned Jerry Lee Lewis in its wake.

Chapter Three

Record Deal

"I knew what I could do, and I knew that if somebody could help me, and put me a record out, I was going to be a big hit."

—Jerry Lee Lewis

In the fall of 1955, Jerry Lee Lewis received some encouragement and inspiration from an unexpected source. He was listening to the radio when he heard an up-and-coming new artist by the name of Elvis Presley performing the song "Blue Moon of Kentucky." The song had some definite country roots, but it also had a jump and jive that was familiar to Lewis. He instinctively realized that this Elvis character was mixing the best of country music and the blues together in what would become termed rockabilly.

Lewis would then be even further encouraged later that year when he was introduced to the sonic sounds of Fats Domino and Little Richard. Both men, of course, played the piano, which in itself was a great source of encouragement for Jerry Lee Lewis. These guys were pounding the keys just like him, and their musical styles were arguably even more rambunctious. Witnessing the careers of these men take off, Lewis got the bright idea to follow in their footsteps. He knew that Elvis had been a lowly truck driver before making it big by way of Sam Phillips of Sun Records. Lewis then quite naturally hoped that Sun Records would cut him the same kind of opportunity.

It was on this rarest of prospects that Lewis, with his father Elmo in tow, piled into a truck and headed off for Memphis. He and his father stayed in a hotel near the record company as Lewis worked up the nerve to audition. The gatekeeper at Sun that he first ran into was producer Jack Clement. Sam Phillips wasn't available for impromptu auditions, but Clement let Lewis play his heart out on a piano for him. Clement liked what he heard and even made a recording of the session. Lewis was no doubt disappointed that he didn't even get to meet Sam Phillips, but he did get Clement to promise that he would play the recordings for Phillips upon his return.

Clement kept his promise, and upon hearing the sounds of Jerry Lee Lewis, Phillips was indeed completely blown away. Phillips would then invite Lewis to the studio on November 14, 1956, so that he could make his first official recordings. Aiding him in this task was a drummer by the name of Jimmy Van Eaton and a guitar player named Roland Janes. These two were veteran session musicians and were used to guiding newcomers to the studio, but they quickly found out that with Jerry Lee Lewis, such a thing was impossible. From the beginning, they had to let Lewis take absolute charge and just try to keep up.

It was a few days after this first recording session was laid down that Jack Clement formally introduced Jerry Lee Lewis to Sam Phillips. Lewis initially wasn't too impressed, describing Sam Phillips as being "stone-faced" and stating that the only time he really seemed to get happy was when he "started talking about money." But one could hardly blame Sam Phillips. He was a businessman surrounded by artists. If he didn't make sure all of the financial arrangements were made, his talent couldn't focus on producing their art. Most artists, after all, are used to thinking of things in the abstract, and many are notoriously bad with money.

One of the first things that Sam Phillips asked young Jerry Lee Lewis was how big of a audience here had a penchant for hurling beer bottles at the live acts. The night Lewis played, it's said that a riot broke out, and the police had to be called in twice to subdue the crowd. Nevertheless, Lewis survived, and soon he was back in the studio to make some more recordings. It was these sessions that would render Jerry Lee Lewis' breakthrough hits— "Whole Lotta Shakin' Goin' On" and "Great Balls of Fire."

On October 6, 1957, a rather conflicted Lewis sat down to record "Great Balls of Fire." It's said that he felt a little bad about the lyrics, thinking that they were too worldly. It seems Jerry Lee Lewis, despite his wild life, couldn't quite shake all of the vestiges of his Christian upbringing. It had suddenly dawned on his skinny shoulders, the great responsibility an artist has as it pertains to influencing young listeners, and he honestly felt a bit guilty for what he perceived as a less-than-moral song. Nevertheless, after some coaxing from Sam Phillips, Lewis finally sat down at the piano and belted out this seminal tune.

On the heels of dropping this "Great Balls of Fire" recording, Jerry Lee Lewis put away his second wife and married his third, Myra Gale Brown, on December 12, 1957. Lewis would court lasting controversy over this union, however, for Myra was not only his cousin, but she was also only 13 years old. Jerry had apparently met Myra during his previous trip home visiting relatives. The young girl caught his eye, and she too was smitten by the then-21-year-old Jerry Lee Lewis. They talked and grew fond of each other, and while Lewis was away performing, they began exchanging frequent phone calls. It seems that all of this long-distance talk led to the fracturing of Jerry's second marriage and the facilitation of his controversial third.

Although today, we are astonished at the age gap between this performer and his new bride. Apparently, in the 1950s in the parts of the Deep South that Lewis hailed from, such marriages were not all that uncommon. Jerry's own sisters, in fact, had married at similar ages. It was a different world in 1950s Louisiana, in which many dropped out of school in their early teens and became hard-working adults at a much younger age. Even so, Lewis was obviously aware of the controversy such a thing would bring outside of his hometown stomping grounds, and as such, he often lied about the girl's age to others.

At any rate, it was shortly after this latest marriage took place that the bouncing ball of energy known as Jerry Lee Lewis once again went on tour. This latest tour was organized by disc jockey and professional promoter Alan Freed. Freed conducted what were termed Big Beat tours for up-and-coming young rock and rollers, and it was in the spring of 1958 that Lewis embarked upon one of these tours, which would take him all across the nation over the span of some 45 days. He was usually the headliner, but occasionally he was the opening act for other big-time artists such as Chuck Berry and Fats Domino. Lewis never liked being the opening act if he could help it since this usually indicated some sort of deference to the major players. Even so, when he was relegated to being the warm-up, he made sure that his performance was so dynamic that the main headliner would have a very hard time competing with it.

Jerry Lee Lewis had renewed his contract with Sam Phillips by this time, which would have him booked with Sun Records all the way to 1963. Yet as hot of an item as Lewis was, no one could foresee the future and the British invasion of new talent to come.

Chapter Five

Fall from Grace

"Either be hot or cold. If you are lukewarm, the Lord will spew you forth from His mouth."

—Jerry Lee Lewis

In the spring of 1958, the King of Rock and Roll—Elvis Presley—had been drafted into the U.S. and shipped off to Germany. This left what seemed to be a wide opening for any other would-be rocker to fill the gap. For a time, Jerry Lee Lewis seemed prepped and primed to take Presley's place as number one.

However, Lewis was far more conflicted about his role as an influencer of young people than Elvis was. Elvis never seemed to think too much about his influence on young people and whether or not it conflicted with any religious sensibilities. Lewis, on the other hand, did—so much so that his deeply ingrained religious convictions would, on occasion, nearly paralyze him with guilt and doubt. At one point, during the Big Beat tour of 1958, an inconsolable Lewis was openly telling his bandmates that he sincerely believed that he was "dragging the audience to hell with me."

The fallout of Jerry's marriage to his young cousin Myra, in the meantime, was growing, and it was having an impact on his latest single, "High School Confidential." In this song, Lewis was trying to capture the energy of a bunch of high school kids, but it could be that listeners were simply grossed out at the prospect considering the young age of his bride. At any rate, his latest song failed to rise to the top, making it only to the twentieth spot on the charts before quickly plummeting to the bottom. Sam Phillips at Sun Records likely thought this was just a fluke, but in reality, it was the beginning of a solid trend.

Lewis would not return to anything near the level of his previous success. Soon, TV shows and radio stations were refusing even to have Jerry Lee Lewis on as he became a kind of contaminated character. As the controversy surrounding his life grew, he eventually told the press that it was none of their business, stating that his marriage was "between [him] and God." Of course, as anyone who's been in the spotlight for any length of time can likely readily attest, the more you dodge reporters and refuse to ask questions, the more questions they will ask.

Despite his evasiveness, Lewis eventually realized that he would have to address the controversy, and he did so on June 9, 1958. He penned a letter for *Billboard* magazine in which he admitted that he had led a "stormy" life. Then, the much more contrite and humbled Jerry Lee Lewis pleaded to his fans that all he ever wanted was to be "worthy" of their "admiration." The pleas did not work.

The best success he had in the next few years was when he recorded a cover of Ray Charles' "What'd I Say" in 1961, which managed to reach as high as 30 on the charts. Ray Charles was another great piano player, most certainly on par with Lewis in many respects. The song had been a fantastic hit for Ray just a couple of years prior, and Jerry was hoping that it would still be able to work some magic for him as well. Even though he only managed to make it in the 30 range on the charts, it was at least a small glimpse of perhaps better things to come. Lewis hoped that this was a sign that his music-listening audience were willing to give him another chance. Unfortunately for Lewis, it was not—at least not yet—and his musical ride was downhill from here.

Lewis did manage to get on Dick Clark's *American Bandstand* in 1962, but the extra exposure didn't seem to make much of a dent. He and Myra in the meantime had produced a son together—Steve Allen—who was born in 1959. Sadly, Steve would perish while Lewis was out on tour, drowning in a backyard swimming pool in 1962. The couple would then have another baby together when their daughter Phoebe was born in 1963. Phoebe made the couple's grief of losing their previous child a little easier, but Lewis was still quite distraught during this period in his life.

As Jerry Lee Lewis continued to struggle with his faltering music career, he would be almost entirely overshadowed by the arrival of a British rock group called the Beatles. Kicking off what would become known as the "British Invasion," the Beatles landed in the United States on February 7, 1964. From here on out, Beatlemania would be the new thing, and the sounds of Jerry Lee Lewis and his 1950s peers would be deemed decidedly old school. It would prove harder and harder for Lewis to find his footing as these new and vibrant musicians from across the pond completely stole the show.

Chapter Six

An Unexpected Return

"Other people—they practice, and they practice. These fingers of mine, they got brains in them. You don't tell them what to do—they do it. God given talent."

—Jerry Lee Lewis

As any chance of success began to rapidly slip away from him, the 1960s would for Jerry Lee Lewis become forever known as his "lost decade." It would not be until the dawning of the 1970s that he would have any chance of recapturing any of the fame and fortune that he had lost, but that doesn't mean that he didn't try. Just as the Beatles were landing in the spring of 1964, Lewis recorded a hyper, hard-driving track called "I'm on Fire," which under normal circumstances might have done quite well. But in the wake of the Beatles, it was hardly noticed at all.

he was down and out, now that he was big time once again, he took her support entirely for granted. She seemed to sense as much, and rather than stay at home and put up with his antics, she filed for divorce.

Unlike his previous divorces, this one was painful for Lewis. It seems that once he was served with divorce papers and knew that Myra was serious, he had genuine remorse. He began to beg for her to reconsider, but Myra, who was well aware of her husband's flagrant infidelity and wild party habits, was unwilling to give him a second chance. Ultimately, the couple were officially divorced in late 1970. This final separation was particularly rough for Lewis since it happened just as his mother became gravely ill with cancer. A few months later, his beloved Mamie would pass away. He had now lost not just one but two women who had played a major part in his life.

occasionally embraced as a unique, flustered moment and easily forgotten. But when one becomes as consistently flustered as Lewis had become, it becomes nothing short of a complete and utter trainwreck. Things got so bad that Lewis was being booed off stage by his own fans. They had come to see a concert, after all, not a drunk and drug-addled man struggling to play his own songs.

Lewis' inebriated antics would then get him into hot water when, on September 29, 1976, he accidentally shot one of his bandmates. The occasion was his 41st birthday, and he was celebrating with his friends at his wife Jaren's residence. He was joking around in his typical drugged-up state when he pulled out a gun and shot at a bottle. The bullet somehow ricocheted and hit his bass player Butch Owens right in the chest. Owens would live to tell the tale, and a few years later, he would sue Jerry for some $400,000, almost as an afterthought. Lewis may have escaped criminal prosecution this time, but after his next drug-fueled adventure, he would not be so lucky.

After giving some thought to his by-then quite reclusive buddy, Elvis Presley, Lewis decided to drive over to the King's residence in Graceland on November 23, 1976. Drunk out of his mind, he accidentally rammed the gates with his car. He then tried to get out of the car and somehow busted his own window in the process. Guards, seeing the bizarre sight of Jerry Lee Lewis, called the police, and Lewis was subsequently hauled away and thrown in jail. Lewis apparently really wanted to see Elvis, but his means of doing so sent him straight to the slammer. His approach was so over the top it seemed more like he was storming a compound than merely paying a visit.

Sadly enough, Elvis would die a year later, ending any future chance of the two coming together as friends and fellow performers.

survive this run-in with death, even though it would take him several weeks to recuperate.

One would think that after such a brush with death, one would take it easy—but not Jerry Lee Lewis. As soon as he had recovered from the surgery, he was back on the road, drinking and partying just as he had done before. Friends and family tried to advise him against it, but he continued his hard-living ways. His estranged wife Jaren, in the meantime, would be found dead in a swimming pool in 1982. Some have tried to suggest some sort of foul play in her death, especially since the couple had just begun official divorce proceedings, but no evidence of this has ever been found.

Even more startling perhaps is the fact that shortly after Jaren's demise, Lewis married his girlfriend, Shawn Stephens, who then also abruptly perished. Lewis married her in August of 1983, only for Shawn to die of an apparent drug overdose a couple of months later. Jerry would then go on to marry one Kerrie McCarver in April of 1984, a marriage which would ultimately last until 2005. Kerrie, who was in her early twenties at the time of the wedding, was a local performer at a place called Hernando's Hideaway. Despite their age difference—or any other differences—the couple professed that they approve. Even before the film was made, he had seen the script and immediately rejected it.

Lewis' personal life was becoming increasingly strained in the meantime as his wife Kerrie sought to exert more control over her husband. The fact that she was reining the wild man in was perhaps not necessarily a bad thing considering his out-of-control escapades of the past, but the fact that she managed to push out many of his loved ones in the process became quite disconcerting. It seems that Kerrie didn't get along with many of the people in Jerry's inner circle and often tried to prevent him from seeing them.

Kerrie then upped her game considerably by becoming her husband's manager. This proved to be devastating for Lewis' career, however, since Kerry was not the best at arranging concert dates, and many potential venues were overlooked in the process. Kerry did have somewhat of an entrepreneurial spirit, though, as was evidenced when she managed to turn her and Jerry's home into a kind of tourist attraction. She periodically opened it up to the public, allowing fans to pay money to take a tour of the premises.

Although Lewis had toned down his wild living to some degree by this point, he had

Conclusion

The last years of Jerry Lee Lewis' life went by fast. Right on the heels of his latest album release—*Mean Old Man*—Lewis began seeing one Judith Brown. She was a family friend and initially presented herself as a kind of caregiver for the ailing and aging Lewis. As was often the case in Lewis' life, however, the two soon became something more than friends, and Judith would ultimately become his seventh and final wife on March 9, 2012.

Lewis' health would continue to decline in the meantime, much of it a mixed result of his previous hard living, coupled with the stone-cold facts of pure and simple advanced age. Jerry Lee Lewis was a fighter, though, and would struggle on until his dying day. That day came on October 28, 2022, when he was 87 years old.

Just prior to his death, Lewis had one final act in mind. He returned to his stomping grounds of Ferriday, Louisiana, and reunited with his televangelist cousin Jimmy Swaggart. Jerry wasn't there to be preached at, however; he was there to play music. He and Jimmy collaborated together on a gospel album called *Jimmy Lee & Jerry Lee: The Boys From Ferriday*. This album focused on themes of forgiveness, faith, and redemption and had Jerry Lee Lewis finally make his return to his gospel roots, resulting in some rather powerful and heartfelt recordings.

Lewis' subsequent funeral, also held in Ferriday, Louisiana, was officiated by none other than Jimmy Swaggart himself. It is indeed fitting that Jerry Lee Lewis made one last return to Ferriday, even as he was making his exit from this world.

Made in the USA
Monee, IL
22 January 2024